Contents

This book is based upon Neal
Teitler's *Know Your Goldfish*. It
has been edited and thoroughly
revised with additional material in
the form of new captions and completely new color photography by
Dr. Herbert R. Axelrod.

ISBN 0-87666-802-3

© 1981 by Dr. Herbert R. Axelrod

All photographs not otherwise
credited are presented through the
courtesy of Midori Shobo, Tokyo,
Japan.

Distributed in the U.S. by T.F.H. Publications, Inc., 211 West
Sylvania Avenue, PO Box 427, Neptune, NJ 07753; in England by
T.F.H. (Gt. Britain) Ltd., 13 Nutley Lane, Reigate, Surrey; in Canada
to the pet trade by Rolf C. Hagen Ltd., 3225 Sartelon Street, Mon-
treal 382, Quebec; in Canada to the book trade by H & L Pet Supplies, Inc., 27 Kingston Crescent, Kitchener, Ontario N28 2T6; in
Southeast Asia by Y.W. Ong, 9 Lorong 36 Geylang, Singapore 14; in
Australia and the South Pacific by Pet Imports Pty. Ltd., P.O. Box
149, Brookvale 2100, N.S.W. Australia; in South Africa by Valid
Agencies, P.O. Box 51901, Randburg 2125 South Africa. Published
by T.F.H. Publications, Inc., Ltd.

The T.F.H. Book of
GOLDFISH

NEAL TEITLER

金魚売（夏姿物売三枚続の内）
初代　豊国筆　文化年間

The Golden Fish

Upon reviewing the history of the goldfish as it has been traced in the works of ancient and modern writers, the hobbyist is confronted with many obscure references. However, if these are considered carefully a fairly clear historical evolution of the goldfish can be revealed. With fact and fiction joining hands as the picture unfolds, we can trace their cultivation for close to a thousand years.

It was during the Tsin Dynasty (265-419 A.D.), some say, that a few red-scaled fish were first observed in China. But to say that these were our present golden-finned friends would be a misrepresentation. It is not until the Sung Dynasty (960-1279 A.D.) that we have any record of the goldfish's first domestication. By then the fish were being reared in ponds as household pets.

During the second Chin Dynasty (1115-1234 A.D.) the "Goldfish Pool" at Peking was being used as a commercial breeding establishment. Indeed, before 1276 A.D. varied colored goldfish were being bred and sold for pets in Hangchow. So popular did they become that during the Ming Dynasty (1368-1643 A.D.) known for its pottery, goldfish were taken from their natural pools and cultivated in aquariums made of clay.

Apparently the Chinese maintained their monopoly on the chin-yii—their word for goldfish—for several hundred years. It is not until 1500 A.D. that we have any record of them in Japan. In 1704 we know that Sato Sanzaemon established a goldfish breeding business at Koriyama, which is still one of the great goldfish centers of the world.

Meanwhile, back in China, three new types of fancy chin-yii were being developed. Around 1590, double-tailed varieties (fantails) were first recorded. In 1621, transparent-scaled varieties were observed; one is depicted on a Chinese plate now in the possession of the British Museum. The publication of the Imperial encyclopedia, *T'u Shu,* in 1726, reveals the first picture of a goldfish lacking the dorsal fin.

Japan's preoccupation with the "golden fish" grew by leaps and bounds as newer varieties were produced and imported. In 1800, the ryukin was imported from the Ryukyu Islands, and at about this time the ranchu arrived from Korea. At a fish farm in Koriyama in 1840 a ryukin was bred with a ranchu, and this cross resulted in the oranda shishigashira.

Mr. K. Akiyama produced the shubunkin in 1900 by crossing two demekins; it was named by Mr. Matsubara. Mr. Akiyama also produced the calico ryukin; it was named by Mr. F. Packard in 1912. The demekin and demeranchu were introduced into Japan from China soon after the end of the Japanese-Chinese War in 1895.

ncient Japanese and Chinese rtworks (opposite, above and llowing two pages) show at goldfish were first mesticated about 1,000 ars ago. Note the goldfish ndor on facing page.

On the other side of the world this natural oddity was also becoming popular. How did it get to Europe and then to America? Many tales were told about this Oriental wonder. In 1691 Petiver wrote the first valid account of this carp-like fish. By 1728 it was well-known in Europe. When Captain Philip Worth presented a large shipment of goldfish to Sir Mathew Decker in 1730, they were well on their way to popularity.

In 1750, the French East India Company brought them into France. The Netherlands in 1753 and Germany in 1780 were both introduced to this aquarist's delight. Edwards mentions double-tailed goldfish in England in 1760. Veil-tails were first bred in France in 1873 and in Germany in 1883, but as early as 1772 Europe had become acquainted with the telescope (demekin) and the dorsal-less types. It was not until after the First World War that the shubunkin reached Europe.

While America probably saw its first goldfish in the early nineteenth century, Admiral Ammon's shipment of 1878 is recognized as the first major import. Before 1889 a goldfish farm was established near Frederick, Maryland; one still exists near there today. In 1899, Mr. Eugene Shireman founded a goldfish farm at Martinsville, Indiana.

The United States can lay claim to developing only one of the many varieties that exist today: the comet. It was apparently produced simultaneously by Hugo Mulertt and the U.S. Fisheries Department in 1881. Anyone who has watched the comet swim will agree that it was aptly named by Mr. Mulertt.

Other varieties are constantly being introduced. The celestial, bubble-eye, pearl-scale, pompon, and outfolded operculum are all twentieth century mutations. To say that this completes the goldfish's history is foolhardy because even today, with every spawning, some new variety may occur.

Fukinagashi, a ryukin or fan-tail.

Yamagato kingyo.

Tetuonaga or black ryukin.

Champion specimens of oranda shishigashira. The lower photograph shows an older champion. The older the fish is, the larger the shishigashira cap.

Above: A velvetyball with narial bouquets. The two fish shown below also have narial bouquets.

Anatomy of the Goldfish

For generations, scientists have been studying evolution and, based on the work of Karl Linnaeus, the Swedish botanist, developing the science of taxonomy. This science has constructed a system of *taxa* (names) to explain the flow of evolution. The goldfish is listed accordingly:

KINGDOM: Animalia
PHYLUM: Chordata
SUBPHYLUM: Vertebrata
CLASS: Osteichthyes
ORDER: Ostariophysi
FAMILY: Cyprinidae
GENUS: *Carassius*
SPECIES: *auratus*

Hence its name *Carassius auratus*.

Osteichthyes pertains to vertebrates (with a backbone) that have a swim bladder, paired pectoral and pelvic fins, an operculum, and possess an endo-skeleton (endo-internal) of bone and cartilage. The Ostariophysi are designated as those Osteichthyes having a series of small bones which connect the swim bladder to the ear. Cyprinidae have toothless jaws; this characterizes more than 2,000 species that belong to the family.

Carassius auratus, the goldfish, has one other member in its genus, the Crucian carp, *Carassius carassius*. The two are distinguished by basic differences in body shape and the convex dorsal fin margin of the Crucian carp versus the goldfish's straight or concave dorsal.

The wild form of the goldfish has between 28 and 31 scales along the lateral line and six scales between the dorsal spine and the lateral line. The goldfish has five sets of fins, and the variation in pairing characterizes different varieties. The swim bladder is an interesting adaptation to water; this is a paired organ in *Carassius auratus*. The swim bladder acts like a ballast tank, causing the fish to rise or sink in the water as it wills.

This fish has five basic senses (sight, smell, taste, lateral line function, and memory) present in varying degrees. Sight is probably the weakest of the goldfish's senses, but coupled with the smell and lateral line adaptations, swift, sharp motions can be made to react to food or other stimuli. The lateral line is a series of pits along the fish's side and is basically an element of touch. When vibrations of the water occur, no matter how slight, a pressure is exerted on this line. Since thermo-sensory nerve endings occur along its length, it is assumed that hot and cold can also be detected by this organ.

To understand the scale groups and coloration of the goldfish, an examination is necessary to explain the reason for their occurrence. Fish have a set of pigment cells called

Shukin goldfish.

Kyonishiki goldfish.

Hibuna, the red crucian carp.

chromatophores which react to temperature, composition of the water, and other environmental factors. Two types which are found in the goldfish are melanophores and xanthophores. In the wild fish an even distribution of both is noted. The yellow and orange types lack the melanophores (black bodies), while in the blue type the xanthophores are absent. Guanine deposited in the cells causes the reflective tissue to be bluish gray in color. A fish's scale group is determined by how much guanine is present at what depth in the skin and scales.

The nomenclature of scale groups developed by the Goldfish Society of Great Britain is the best available:

METALLIC: One that has a lot of guanine and is, therefore, as highly reflective as polished metal.

MATT: The term used to describe fish having a translucent or flat coloration. No matter how closely you examine them, no reflective tissue can be found, not even in the eye orbit, which is an intense black.

NACREOUS: A hybrid of the first two, showing signs of both. Some scales, organs, or other areas might show a concentration of guanine-laden reflective tissue.

CALICO: Originally referred to nacreous fish but is now used to describe a fish of any group which has three or more colors scattered over the body haphazardly, usually including blue. The better calico has regions of intense blue scales.

Scaled and scaleless are useless terms because they are not exact enough, do not explain the hybrid type, and are improper since all goldfish have scales.

A silver goldfish.

Edonishiki.

Yamagata goldfish.

The famed tosakin, or goldfish in Tosa, with the long, upheld tail. The drawing below shows the ideal conformation and flow as the fish swims.

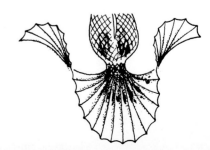

The ranchu goldfish, which is also known as the lionhead, bramblehead or shetau. It has a heavy growth on the head and no dorsal fin. The fish shown below has the growth covering the eyes.

1
Oranda

2
Lionhead

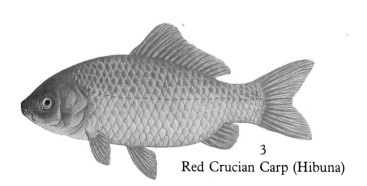

3
Red Crucian Carp (Hibuna)

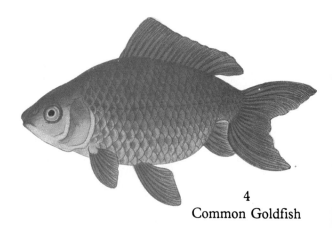

4
Common Goldfish

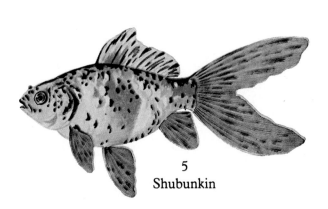

5
Shubunkin

6
Black Moor

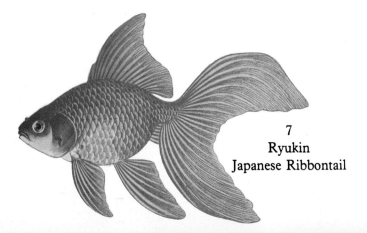

7
Ryukin
Japanese Ribbontail

Some strains of goldfish: 1 Oranda; 2 Lionhead; 3 Red Crucian Carp, Hibuna; 4 Common goldfish of Japan, Wakin; 5 Shubunkin; 6 Black Moor; 7 Japanese Ribbontail, Ryukin.

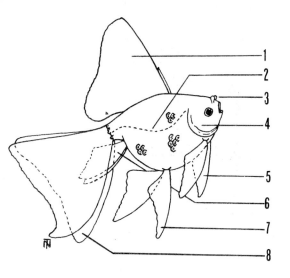

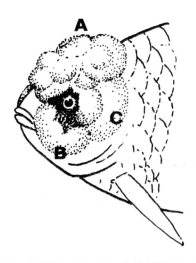

The Varieties of Goldfish

There are many varieties of goldfish. Considering the number of variations in fins, color, body shape, etc., that are possible, the number would appear astronomical. Fortunately, however, the combinations accepted as valid varieties are small when compared to this theoretical number. All goldfish varieties existing today stem from the original stocks developed by Chinese, Korean, and Japanese breeders.

Names are a hard thing to pin down. Each culture, and sometimes regions in that culture, calls the same fish by different names. Oriental breeders look for different features than do those in the western world. It is because of this that some of their names have no English translation. The Chinese use the name dragon to refer to types for which we find no basis. In contrast, the American and British cannot even agree on common English names.

Taking into account contemporary nomenclature, anatomy, and genetics, as well as general descriptiveness, I have set down names which I feel fit the recognized types. Before describing them I will try to explain the recognized variations which when combined form the established breeds.

Color

As previously noted, the depth and intensity of the guanine layer will determine the scale group in which the fish is placed. The chromatophores which are distributed above the guanine, over the skin, determine the coloration. Often these cells expand or contract under visual or nervous stimuli, allowing intensity and sometimes color to change. Darkness tends to cause the chromatophores to expand, thereby amplifying the fish's color. Besides the melanophores (black) and the xanthophores (yellow-orange), deep orange and violet coloring cells have been found. Currently blue is being examined closely to discover if it could be another type.

Fish coloring varies according to the number and size of the chromatophores present. Black, brown, and the wild green are caused by different combinations of the black and yellow pigment cells. Blue goldfish occur in two ways. The blue can be caused by a large amount of guanine and the absence of orange, with some black, or by the black pigmentation lying further down in the skin, with little or no guanine present.

Red or orange specimens occur when few or no black chromatophores are present. Silver or white specimens occur when no pigmentation appears in the skin and only guanine is present. An albino lacks pigment everywhere, including the eyes, which are pink. It should be noted that

Genealogical chart showing goldfish evolution.

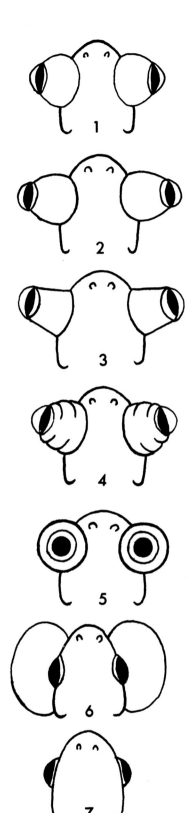

an albino goldfish is not white but pale orange in color. The late Professor Shishan C. Chen noted that no albino goldfish had appeared up to the time of his famous paper in 1925. Today, albino types of most varieties are being raised everywhere.

Almost all, if not all, types of pigment cells and kinds of reflecting tissues present in domesticated goldfish occur in wild specimens. In the latter, however, the cells are distributed more evenly and rarely in so great a concentration as to produce red, orange, blue, or other colored spots. The color cells and reflecting layers in the wild form are so distributed that the fish is gray, dull olive, silvery white, or shades of these in various parts of its body. So, in a sense, the domesticated goldfish has nothing new in terms of color that the parent wild form did not have. However, through change of the genetic material that governs the distribution and concentration of pigment cells, nature has altered the goldfish to produce our brightly colored domesticated varieties.

Finnage

This is an over-all term used to describe the five sets of fins which appear on the fish. Variation in finnage occurs basically in three ways: by doubling or pairing of caudal and anal fins, by their absence (mainly with reference to the dorsal fins), and by an increase in length (all fins, especially caudals).

CAUDAL OR TAIL FIN: The caudal fin varies greatly among the many varieties. This structure consists of a flat membrane supported by fin rays. It develops from a single tail (two-lobed) to the doubled or bilaterally-paired fins

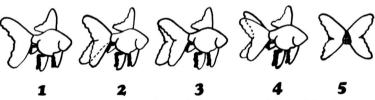

Variation in the Goldfish tail. English names are followed by Japanese translation.

1. Singletail/*Funa-wo*
2. Tripod tail/*Tsumami-wo*
3. Webtail/*Mitsu-wo*
4. Double tail/*Yotsu-wo*
5. Butterfly tail/*Kujaku-wo*

VARIATION IN GOLDFISH EYES
1. *Spheroid*
2. *Ovoid*
3. *Truncated Cone*
4. *Segmented Sphere*
5. *Celestial*
6. *Bubble-eye*
7. *Normal*

Japanese standards recognize these ten tail forms.

(four-lobed). In prize fish the double caudals should be separated all the way to the base or root of the tail, of equal size (especially the lobes), and without permanent folds.

ANAL FIN: As in the caudal, the anal can develop into long or short, single or double types. Double-tail (fan-tail) varieties must have double anals, and they should be of equal size.

DORSAL FIN: When considering the dorsal one rule holds true: it should be all there or there should be no trace at all. The breeds lacking the dorsal should have a smooth back covered evenly with scales, with no vestigial stump showing. A variety with a dorsal should keep it erect, having no folds or breaks evident. In the highly prized veil-tail a sure sign of a good fish is its extremely high dorsal standing like a sail against the wind.

PELVIC AND PECTORAL FINS: These fins also vary in size and shape according to the breed. All of these should be paired and straight, having a symmetrical appearance.

Body Shape

Observation of the many pictures in this book indicates the drastic variations in body shape. It is startling to realize that the very short-bodied veil-tail is an indirect mutation from the long-bodied common goldfish. One "must" for any good specimen is that it must be symmetrical and not distorted.

Head

The hooded goldfish varieties are becoming more popular than ever; they can, therefore, be found in most large pet shops. A good growth does not usually appear until at least the third year. Head shape also varies from pointed to blunt (or square). Oriental breeders have in the past placed more emphasis on this than have those in the West. Head shape is important and it should be taken into account according to the variety.

Other Mutations

Globe or telescope eyes occur and form distinctive types. Nasal growths have been propagated to form another breed. In some fish the bony operculum is affected so another type has come into being.

Varieties

A general rule applied to describe the origin of the many breeds is as follows: Chinese breeders select for grotesque shapes and appearance; the Japanese select for that which is graceful, flowing, and esthetically pleasing. The names I have chosen from the past writings are those which best describe their types.

Hibuna, the red crucian carp.

The red telescope oranda.

An oranda with narial bouquet.

A sanshoku-demekin calico telescope.

A beautiful aka-demekin or red telescope. Aka is the Japanese word for red.

Single-tail Fish

This is the least modified of ornamental goldfish, having a body shape and fin structure similar to that of the wild type. These were the first cultivated goldfish bred by the Chinese. They are the easiest variety to breed and the hardiest. Outdoors in a pool they grow to 12 inches in two years. After a number of years, lake-grown "commons" can grow close to two feet. A calico, matt, or nacreous common is usually called a shubunkin.

Comet (tetsugyo)

The comet is a long-finned common goldfish said to have originated about 1880 in United States Government ponds on the Mall in Washington, D.C. Hugo Mulertt, a pioneer American breeder, may have also originated this fish at about the same time; at any rate, he gave it its name.

The body of a fine comet is more elongated than that of the common goldfish and the single tail-fin as long as, or preferably longer than, the body. All other fins are at least twice the length of those of the common goldfish and often, and preferably, much longer.

Like the common goldfish it is a hardy fish well able to stand cold winters outdoors, and it is a prolific and efficient breeder. It is a graceful, active fish and its fins do not seem as delicate and subject to disease as do other long-finned varieties. It can reach a length of 20 inches but ordinarily reaches 14 inches in outdoor pools. It makes an excellent ornamental pond fish as it is better able to escape small boys, cats, and other predators than can the double-tailed, short-bodied varieties.

London and Bristol shubunkins

These fish are recognized solely as shubunkins or calicoes of other types. The London shubunkin resembles the common fish in body and finnage. As mentioned previously, it is basically a calico type of the matt or nacreous fish. The Bristol shubunkin resembles the comet in body shape and long square finnage. In most respects it is like the Goldfish Society's single-tail variety except that its tail is square at the ends instead of rounded.

A long-tailed crucian carp.

A beautiful comet goldfish.

A calico fringe-tail.

A champion-quality stock of Nagoya goldfish called "jikin," or peacocktail goldfish. The strain is very well fixed and breeds true.

This red telescope eye is a common goldfish sold in most aquarium shops outside the Orient. Red telescopes are usually very hardy and are bred locally. The United States, Canada, England, Australia and New Zealand have thriving goldfish hatcheries. Israel began in 1980 to produce some of the more colorful goldfish, because the Israelis are able to feed their goldfish with live shrimp which they catch only a few miles from their goldfish farm. Feeding live brine shrimp or daphnia makes an immense difference in the size and color of goldfish.

Telescope eyes on goldfish are very common, and many color varieties have been bred with telescope eyes. The almost pure black specimen shown below is a champion in Japan.

A maruko goldfish.

A Chinese narial bouquet.

A shubunkin.

Double-tail fish

Ribbon-tail (fan-tail, ryukin)

A short body and fairly long finnage typify this group. Smaller finnage as found in the commercial fan-tail is really an inferior form of ryukin. Poor culling results in fish with longer bodies and short fins as found in the wakin. The longer the body of a fish, the more chance you have of obtaining a single-tail in your future spawns. Most often the good specimens will grow to about ten inches in three years.

According to its recorded history, the ryukin originally came from the Ryukyu Islands. The best ribbon-tails have deeply divided tails (four lobes), two anals, and a complete division of the two caudals down to the base.

Veil-tail (twin-tail)

High dorsals, long finnage, and "square cut" caudals make this fish the aristocrat of the goldfish family. Good specimens are hard to come by and command high prices. In all cases the caudal and anals are doubled and must be divided down to the base; they must be symmetrical. This is one of the least hardy of the varieties, so care must be taken when handling them. Their short body and long finnage slow them down, making them easy prey for outdoor predators. Many times their tail grows too long and must be trimmed (tail-docking), a procedure recommended by the noted goldfish expert Mr. J. W. Anderson.

An excellent specimen may breed only one or two squared tails, so care must be taken in order to raise them. A good sign of a good fish is one that has a very high dorsal with extremely long finnage. The square tail comes later or can be bred out in later generations.

Globe-eye (telescope, demekin, chair-lay)

For years these fish have been called "telescope," a name which is very inappropriate. The protruding eyes which characterize this group are anything but telescopic. Body shape should be short and the fins symmetrically paired. Eye shape varies in four ways. A good specimen has long fins and a well-divided ribbon-tail. Coloration varies immensely, creating the varying types of demekins which the Japanese have named.

Black Moor (kuro demekin)

A type of globe-eye, this fish is solid black in color, preferably with a matt covering. Many Moors turn color later in age, since black is the least stable of goldfish colors. Mr. Anderson states that a Moor with a white or silvery belly will remain black, while one with a brassy or golden belly will turn orange later in its life.

27

Pearl-scale (chee-lun)

Of all the modern varieties (those produced after 1900) this has proved extremely popular. Its body is extremely short and round, approaching a softball in size and shape. The scales seem like hemispheres or half pearls which have been pasted onto the fish's body. Good specimens have large scales and short square finnage. Young fry with ribbon-tail caudals can later develop into fish with square veil-tails.

It is interesting to note that when a scale is injured and falls off the new scale is of the normal flat type, but this does not affect the fish's breeding ability to transfer genes for good pearl-scaled development to its progeny.

Oranda

Goldfish hobbyists and breeders are all agreed that the oranda is a fish universal in appeal. A good specimen has a well-developed hood (a puffy growth of the skin in the head region), long paired finnage, a high dorsal, and a well-developed short body. Oranda shishigashira is used mainly to refer to the type of oranda which has only a well-developed cap. The azumanishiki is the Japanese name for a calico oranda, a name widely used all over the world. Some orandas grow to 12 inches and appear to do well when wintered outdoors. Top specimens, however, if more than five years old, should be taken indoors during the winter period.

Bramblehead (lionhead, ranchu, shetau)

The Bramblehead has a short round body, short finnage, no dorsal, a double anal fin, and a warty growth on the head. Specimens should have no dorsal vestiges, and the back can either be slightly rounded with caudal straight out or fairly flat with the caudal peduncle and caudals at a 45° inclination downward. Three hood types are recognized by the Japanese: tokin—growth only on cap; okame—swollen-cheeked; shishigashira—full hood on cap, cheeks, and opercular region.

Pompon (yeung-kau)

The variety recognized today lacks the dorsal. (The Japanese type, hanafusa, has it, and many people have incorrectly called it Pompon, but a more apt name advocated by Professor Chen is narial bouquet.) All finnage is paired, the body is short, and the nasal appendages are folded many times to form tufts. As with all goldfish lacking a dorsal, short finnage is preferred so that the fish are able to move and balance with some ease.

Celestial (deme ranchu, chiu-tien ngarn, chotengan)

This grotesque variation of the globe-eye was probably

A blue oranda.

A white shukin.

A chotengan celestial.

The ryukin goldfish, also known as the fantail. The specimen to the left is a young fish about two years old, while the fish shown below is about five years old.

produced in Korea sometime after 1780, winding up in Japan about 1901. Characteristic of this breed are the up-turned eyes encased in a hard bulbous orbit. These fish, which lack a dorsal fin, are extremely delicate and can be easily injured. All sharp objects should be removed from the tank because they are able to see only upward. Feeding with prepared fish foods which will not cloud the water or decay rapidly is especially necessary for this variety.

Bubble-eye

Another grotesque Chinese production, the bubble-eye is extremely delicate. The eyeball is quite normal, but large fluid-filled sacs protrude from the eye socket, causing the eyeball to turn up almost as much as does the celestial's. Good specimens have a short body, paired finnage (short), no dorsal, and extremely large fluid sacs equal to each other in size. This variety was first described by Professor Chen and is believed to be a twentieth century mutation.

An albino goldfish.

Other types

The outfolded operculum (faan si) is a popular Chinese fish which is seldom seen outside of China. Good specimens have a high dorsal, good ribbontail, long paired finnage, and operculum folded back on both sides, exposing the gills.

Albinos are now being bred in most varieties. According to Chen no one had seen an albino prior to 1925. The American breeders have developed strains that are available in limited quantities.

Other varieties not yet mentioned include: the nymph, a single-tailed ryukin; the blue Moor; the brown or chocolate variety; and the red cap oranda which is all white with red only on the shishigashira cap.

One of the newer and more popular goldfish is the red head or the red cap which is an oran-da shishigashira with a white body and a red head. Raspberry head, strawberry head and other similar designations have been applied to this fish. Recently a white cap (see lower photo on facing page) has been developed.

Water bubble-eyes, or frogheads as they are called in Japanese, have been developed in recent years. They are anything but beautiful, though beauty has long since left the priorities of Oriental goldfish breeders. The black froghead shown to the left is so topheavy that it must rest in this position, with its head on the gravel.

Setting Up the Aquarium

Selecting the tank

When starting out to buy the aquarium, keep in mind that it is to serve as a *home* for your goldfish and do not consider it as just a fancy decoration. Goldfish require more space than most varieties of pet fish. To begin with, a safe rule to follow is to allow one inch of fish (not including the tail) per gallon of water. Since the goldfish needs a good supply of oxygen, no less than 30 square inches of surface area is required for each inch of fish. Surface area can be determined by multiplying the length of the tank by its width. Gallon capacity can be found by using the formula:

$$\frac{\text{Length} \times \text{Width} \times \text{Height}}{231}$$

All measurements are in inches.

Now that we have determined the size, let's consider the shape of the tank. The aquarium best suited to goldfish is one which is rectangular. Squat bowls or turtle bowls, while not bad in a pinch, should be avoided. Glass bowls shaped like globes or like a layer-cake on its side are not too good either, but if you are determined to have one remember this: under no circumstances fill the bowl *above* the widest portion, usually its half-way point. While most of these glass bowls are inexpensive, in the long run they cause more trouble than the saving is worth.

Many beginners decide to start small and then get larger tanks. If you can afford only a small tank, try to spend a little more and buy at least a ten-gallon aquarium. I have observed novices count fish size and then buy a five-gallon tank. Before long they see some other fish that they would like to have but make the sad discovery that their tank will not hold them. If in doubt, always buy the larger tank. If you have a choice between two tanks with the same capacity, differing only in length and width, choose the one with the larger surface area.

Choose an aquarium made by a well-known firm. You will then have a tank that will stand up under use. Above all, remember that a reputable dealer who sells well-known brands is a dealer you can rely on to advise you.

When you have gotten your tank home and set in place, your job has just begun. Fill the tank with about two inches of water and wait for half an hour. Examine the tank, checking for any small leaks. Small drips are usually sealed by water pressure at that point inside the aquarium. Larger leaks must be cared for *immediately*. Empty the tank, let it dry, and then get to work with a good silicone cement. The key to solving most tank problems is experimentation: try some established method and then judge for yourself.

How many millions of children got started with a few goldfish in a goldfish bowl? What a terrible torture for the goldfish!

A beautiful comet.

Edonishiki.

Some of the most commonly used goldfish products are available in pre-packaged units that are more economical than buying the individual items separately.

The proper conditioning of the water is very important in goldfish management; many products that help to insure good environmental control are available as aids to the hobbyist.

Location

The placement of your tank should be carefully considered. No direct sunlight must hit it. A tank staying too long in the sun turns green with algae quickly and presents a problem. Indirect sunlight or artificial lighting for about six hours a day is enough. If there are plants in the tank, then the lighting should be for at least ten hours. With plants you can gauge the amount of light needed because if they do not get enough they will begin to turn brown.

Gravel — yes or no?

Gravel is a big "if" in keeping goldfish. If you decide to use gravel, its size is extremely important. Bits that are too large cause accumulation of dirt and wastes which can result in disease. Bits that are too small cause bacteria to form, blackening the packed bottom layer. What is the right size? From past experience I would say those bits of gravel about three-eighths to one-fourth inch in size are about best. One and a half pounds of this size gravel for each gallon of tank capacity are more than ample.

I must warn any novice that goldfish do not keep the best of company with plants and gravel. This fish is a scavenger and will rearrange the bottom of the tank at will. One time I discovered 20 pounds of gravel moved to one corner of the tank in less than two days. You can become quite disturbed if after carefully planting and aquascaping a new tank you see all your effort gone to waste.

Water

Most water is chlorinated and/or fluoridated and therefore must be conditioned. There are chemicals on the market for this purpose, but letting the water stand for 24 hours is a satisfactory method. pH or alkalinity-acidity of the water is not an important factor with goldfish. After the fish have lived for a while in the water, it usually becomes slightly acid.

Water hardness, while important for tropical fishes, can vary with goldfish. It should be noted, however, that in commercial fisheries before the fish are shipped they are conditioned by being placed in a pond filled with spring water which is hard and slightly alkaline.

Once your tank is filled, don't under any circumstances move it.

Pumps

The pump is one item which will be determined by your individual set-up. Here you have a wide choice in styles, types, and capacity. Two basic types are available: the vibrator or diaphragm pump and the piston pump.

Vibrator pumps are less expensive and have mechanical failures less often than do the piston pumps. This pump

1

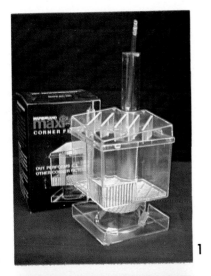

2

works by way of a rubber diaphragm which is actuated by a mechanism similar to that operating an electric bell or buzzer. For a beginner, this is probably the best. Later on, however, you may want to set up a series of five or more tanks. With a system this large, the vibrator pump is inadequate and a piston pump will be needed.

The piston pump operates through a motor system. A magnet inside changes with the AC current, causing a small rod to rotate. This rod is connected to a wheel by way of a belt, and the wheel is connected to a plunger. The plunger, which is inside a cylindrical case, moves up and down, forcing air down into the cylinder and out through a connection to the air line. Most piston pumps must be cleaned and oiled regularly according to the maker's directions.

Here, as always, if the pump is purchased from a reputable dealer and is one made by a well-known company, you stand a good chance that your pump will cause few or no problems. Most economy pumps create nothing more than breakdowns. While a pump with a guarantee may cost more, the cost is low when you consider how long it will be in use.

Filters for tanks housing goldfish come in many different forms. Beginners can rely on their pet dealers to provide good advice about which filtration systems will be best for their set-ups. Shown here are: 1. inside corner filter 2. inside sponge-type filter 3. vibrator air pump.

3

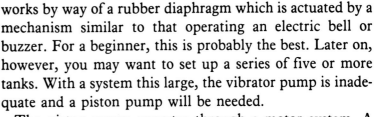

Three different views of water bubble-eyes.

Filters

Several types can be recommended for the goldfish tank. The outside power filter is perhaps the best as it is the easiest to clean and takes up no room in the aquarium, which is important in tanks of less than 15-gallon capacity. When the floss which acts as a filter becomes dirty, the air line is stopped and the floss is replaced. Thus, after only a few minutes of interrupted service, the filter is back at work. The outside filter does have one disadvantage, however. If the water level drops too low, it ceases operation.

In many tanks a corner filter is used in conjunction with an outside filter. While the outside filter cleans up most wastes along the bottom of the aquarium, the bottom filter will remove most floating wastes. It is easy to clean but it must be removed from the tank to do so. When you replace the floss be extremely careful that no fibers remain outside the cover. I have seen this carelessness cause the death of many a goldfish: when the fish sees the glistening floss it tugs at it and either chokes on it or swallows it. The chief fault of the corner filter is that it takes up space in the tank.

With any of these filters, set up and cleaning is an easy task. The charcoal that is purchased from pet shops is often dusty and should be rinsed. Place the charcoal in a pail under a faucet. Run the water until the overflow is crystal clear, making sure that you agitate the charcoal four or five times. A more efficient method is to use a sixteenth-inch mesh net. Fill the net three-quarters full of charcoal and agitate it under running water by pressing up the bottom several times. When you see that a clear flow of water is running through, you will know that the charcoal is clean. Wash the filter and place this clean charcoal in it, filling it a third of the way. Add floss to the two-thirds mark, and your filter is ready to operate.

Undergravel filters are often used in conjunction with power filters, especially in larger aquaria. They are slotted plastic plates that go under the gravel layer. Your dealer will gladly show you the best type of filter for your aquarium set-up.

Air stone

An air stone is another useful item because it allows more water to be exposed to the air. Air stone bubbles do not add oxygen to the water directly; they stir up the water, causing a faster exchange of oxygen at the surface with the carbon dioxide in the water.

Valves

When you set up an air system of more than one filter or aerator, you will have to consider the valve system. The two types available include one which is a series of valves with one inflow and many outflows and one composed of a series of three-way valves. I have tested both and prefer the former. All the valve controls are on one gang valve, making it easy to control and adjust each unit to the desired air outflow.

1. Undergravel filter. 2. Power filter; power filters contain small water pumps and therefore do not require a separate air pump in order to operate.

A magnificent specimen of a celestial goldfish which the Japanese call "chotengan." The fish shown to the left is a nice specimen, only a few years old, but if it continues to grow this way will soon be a champion.

Champion ranchu lionhead goldfish from Japan. The larger the head growth, the older the fish.

Ryukin or fantail goldfish are by far the most common of the "fancy" goldfish which are now available on the market. These champion fish from Japan portray the ideal form of the ryukin.

Other accessories

The goldfish hobbyist will also find these things useful: a dip tube or siphon tube, a feeding ring, a net, and a thermometer.

As for the siphon tube, I have found the best way to clean dirt from the tank is with a length of ordinary tubing. Cut a piece of air hose about four feet long. Attach it to a wooden dowel, which should be about six inches longer than the depth of your tank, so that one end of the tubing sticks out about half an inch beyond the end. Place this end in the water and either suck up water or lay the entire piece of tubing under the water until all the air escapes and it is filled. Put your finger on the loose end and set it in a bucket *lower* than the bottom of the tank. Now move the other end along the bottom of your tank at about a 60° angle until all waste products are sucked up. Anything too large to pass through the tube should be avoided and picked up later with a net. The siphon flow is stopped simply by lifting the tip of the hose out of the tank. Aged water is then added to the tank, replacing the quantity siphoned out.

A feeding ring set in one place keeps the food in the same spot, training the fish to know where it will be found. The net, of course, is used to handle the fish, moving them from one tank to another or into medicated water for treatment. An inexpensive thermometer is needed as a guide to checking aged water that is being added to the tank or the water in a tank to which the fish are being moved. A heater is not necessary unless you intend to raise fry.

Introducing the fish

Once your tank has been washed and rinsed with salt and all the necessary things have been added to it (including plants if you so desire), check the temperature, comparing it with the water the fish are now in. If your water has been properly aged (or chemically treated) and the temperature variation of the water is 5°F or less, you may add your goldfish and sit back and admire your creation.

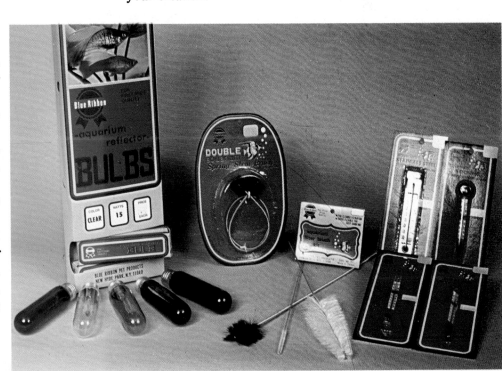

Above: *Air-releasers come in a number of different forms, including porous stones and perforated tubings; they work off an air pump to provide valuable aeration.* Right: *Bulbs for incandescent reflectors, filter brushes, various types of thermometers—just a few of the many useful but inexpensive aquarium accessories available at pet shops.*

Your aquarium store will have some very beautiful aquarium set-ups to show you. They can easily suit the decor of your home or office. Photo courtesy of Werther Paccagnella.

Plants and Gravel

Except for show purposes, most goldfish aquarists discourage the use of gravel and plants. But for those who can't be discouraged, I mention here those plants best able to stand abuse. These varieties are all good oxygenators and are to be found in most pet shops. When buying plants, look for those which are a vivid green, upright, not wilted, and, last but not least, with few or no brown-tipped leaves. As a guide, the various plants have been divided into three general groups: rooted, bunched, and floaters.

Rooted

These do best when planted and the roots are allowed to sprout and settle. *Vallisneria, Sagittaria,* and Amazon swords are the three best for the goldfish aquarium. All of these send out new plants by means of runners. Under good growing conditions (usually not with goldfish) they will multiply rapidly, producing dense jungles of underwater growth. *Vallisneria* comes in many forms and shapes. It is thin and tall, sometimes twining like a corkscrew. It is an excellent oxygenator. It varies in height from six inches to several feet and in width is about one-quarter of an inch. This plant is unusually hardy and thrives under even extreme conditions.

Sagittaria resembles *Vallisneria* in size and shape. Its leaves are slightly broader and, while tougher, are more brittle. Usually it multiplies rapidly and supplies a good deal of oxygen. Once *Sagittaria* begins to brown, cut off the tips or, if necessary, the whole leaf. In most aquaria *Sagittaria* roots easily, spreading out to obtain a firm foothold.

Sword plants, especially the Amazon variety, are as close to ideal goldfish aquarium plants as one can hope to get. They establish themselves easily and, once set, multiply at a slow but steady pace. With good lighting they turn a luxuriant green and make an attractive addition to the tank. No matter how much the goldfish work on them, sword plants seem to be able to withstand their abuse.

Bunched

This group is always to be found where goldfish are bred and raised. Outdoors nothing can compare with them. In a tank they can prove useful, but they are also a hazard. The bunch plants usually do not have true roots and reproduce by means of branches forming off the main stem. They are quite brittle, and with active fish they may end up as a pile of rotting plant fragments.

Elodea has a main stem which grows to anywhere from four inches to four feet. The leaves form whorls, a circle around the stem, and are thin, flat, and pointed at the tip. Goldfish eat the leaves readily and can strip the stem in a

Vallisneria.

Amazon Sword plant.

matter of minutes. Scientific studies on plant respiration have shown *elodea* to be one of the best oxygenators. Old growth tends to be brown and should be cut off. Cuttings of the stems will form new plants.

Cabomba, popular outdoors, has only mild success inside. It is composed of very fine fan-like leaves usually paired around the stem. It is quite brittle, and goldfish have a tendency to thrash it to bits. In spite of these problems, *Cabomba* is internationally famous as an ideal breeding plant. For an unusual effect, try the red variety.

Ambulia is a fairly recent introduction. Its color varies between green and red; it is sometimes mistaken for *Cabomba.* More careful examination will show it to be more dense and rubbery in texture. Under the right growing conditions it fares better than *Cabomba,* even in tanks.

Floaters

Of the many types of floating plants only four will be mentioned here. *Azolla, Salvinia, Riccia,* and duckweed are the most popular and easy to acquire. In general, the floating plants have roots, are flat, and multiply quickly. They require plenty of light and more than ample growing area. If they run out of spreading room they tend to double up and rise out of the water.

Azolla is native to the southern states of the U.S. and is found mainly in bog-like areas. Its colors range anywhere from bright green to deep crimson. In appearance it resembles miniature spinach or evergreen leaves approximately half an inch in length. As with most floaters, *Azolla* requires a lot of sun.

Salvinia is considered by many to be the star of floating plants. Besides giving shade in ponds, it provides a vegetable food source for goldfish. *Salvinia* is oval in shape with fine hairs extending up from its leaves to form a moss-like texture.

Riccia is another plant which requires intense sunlight. It is a vivid green sponge-like mass which intertwines while floating just beneath the surface. In some cases, aquarists have rid ponds of *Riccia* because it looks something like a stringy variety of algae.

Duckweed or *Lemna* appears in dense numbers on ponds. In general, it looks like a miniature version of the oval-shaped *Salvinia.* However, it lacks *Salvinia's* fine hairs and grows in separate leaves or groups of three and four, while *Salvinia* leaves lie on the same stem in groups of seven and up. Duckweed is known all over the world because it establishes itself easily in streams and ponds. Some hobbyists have noticed that the leaves when eaten by goldfish tend to have a slight laxative effect.

Sagittaria.

Salvinia.

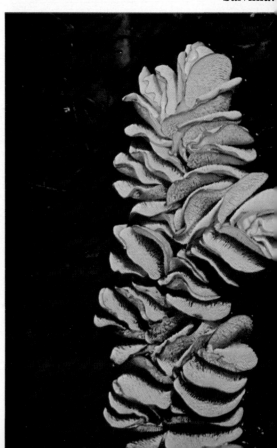

*This beautiful aquarium is part of a bookcase. It is suitable for both tropical fishes and goldfish.
Photo courtesy of Werther Paccagnella.*

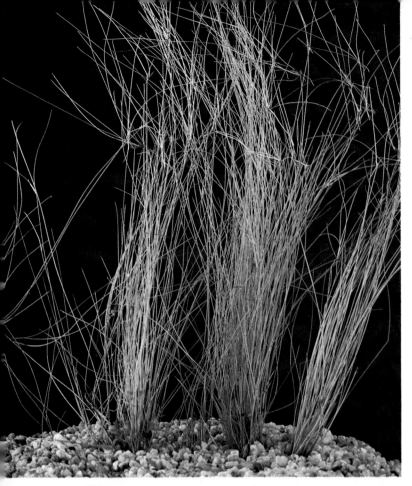

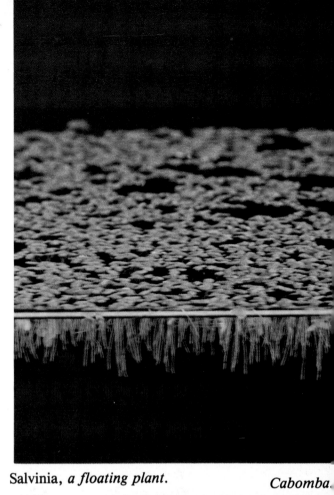

Hairgrass.

Anacharis, or elodea.

Salvinia, *a floating plant.*

Cabomba.

Ludwigia.

Gravel

Gravel when purchased is usually not clean. To clean it, use the cleaning method for charcoal discussed in the section on filters. Make sure that any gravel is washed thoroughly before it is put into the aquarium because the scum its dust will form on the surface is unsightly and hard to remove. The gravel should be placed in cleaned flower pots or behind a barrier. A strong salt solution can be used to clean the pots and other equipment—be sure to carefully rinse it off, of course.

The flower pot method is an efficient way of setting up your tank. Plants which need treatment can then be removed easily, while re-planting will not disturb the water. My experience is that goldfish will not bother potted plants as readily as they do those planted directly in gravel.

The barrier method is perhaps the best, and it works two ways: it keeps the plants and gravel safe, and it makes clean-up easier. Use a sheet of glass or Plexiglas cut to fit the inside length of the aquarium and with holes perforating the outside edges. Place this vertically about four inches from the rear of the tank to serve as a partition. Behind it place the gravel and arrange the plants. The holes will allow an exchange of gases between the two areas, but they should be too small to give the goldfish access to the plants. When the plants are well-rooted, flourishing, and better able to withstand the fish's abuse, this barrier can, if desired, be removed.

If the usual method of laying gravel is used, slope it down toward the front. With the barrier method or with the plants in pots, water can be poured directly into the area where there is no planting. If not, newspaper should be laid over the gravel, a saucer placed on top of it, and the water poured slowly onto the saucer until the tank is filled. If this method is used, the plants, of course, will not be added until all the water is in and the newspaper carefully removed.

Goldfish are hardy fish and can be kept outside in small goldfish pools as well as in an aquarium.

Feeding

There are many different foods available for goldfish; most are inexpensive and easy to obtain. The greater the variety, the more active and colorful your fish will become. Dried and/or pelleted foods, frozen foods, mixed pastes, and live foods are all available. Nothing, in my opinion, beats the last.

Dried foods that are high in starch content tend to cloud the water. New flake foods have been developed which do not foul the tank as readily, and the fish seem to find them appetizing. Shrimp pellets are high in animal matter and have a sharp smell easily detected by the fish. While dried foods have their use, they should not be fed to the exclusion of frozen or live foods. Paste mixtures are made up with different foods like liver, spinach, and egg. Freeze-dried and deep-frozen foods are also available in a wide variety of types at your pet dealer.

Live foods should form the foundation of your feeding schedule. They provide goldfish with foods similar to those they eat in their natural surroundings. Again the choice is great, giving you complete freedom to choose the one best suited to your requirements.

Daphnia

These small crustaceans are also known as water fleas. If you are adventurous, you can search for them in nearby lakes and ponds. It is a food, however, that should be fed in moderation because its chitinous shell acts as a laxative.

If a successful culture can be established, you have a ready supply of live food. Start the culture by placing about an inch of rich organic soil into a jar of stagnant water and letting it stand in the sun for several days. A good algal growth is necessary; it can be stimulated by the addition of some nitrate and phosphate. When the water is ready, add some daphnia. Give them at least a week to establish themselves. It is best to raise several cultures simultaneously because fluctuations and constant use will deplete the original culture.

Brine shrimp

Whole books have been written on this tiny crustacean. They inhabit the Great Salt Lake as well as other areas of high salt concentration and have brought into being a thriving industry. They can be purchased live from most pet shops or can be grown from eggs at home.

Establish a culture by taking a bottle like a cider or wine jug and cutting off the bottom. The tightly corked bottle is then turned upside down and an aerator stone placed in the neck. Salt water in a concentration of about 12 ounces of salt per gallon of water is added. Many aquarists add two

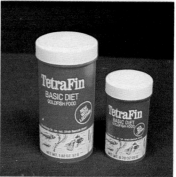

1 and 2. Prepared dried foods. 3. algicidal preparation. 4. aggregate used to provide a colorful bottom for the tank.

Photos by Akira Sugi.

【東】

玉誉

親魚の部　大関東
川辺保之氏持魚

大恵

2才魚の部　大関東
細谷竜三郎氏持魚

大光山

当才魚の部　大関東
三谷正友氏持魚

金魚銘鑑

第8回全国東錦品評大会

日本東錦協会

撮影・杉　彰

【西】

浅錦

親魚の部　大関西
浅沼好三氏持魚

大光山

2才魚の部　大関西
三谷正友氏持魚

龍

当才魚の部　大関西
細谷竜三郎氏持魚

A page from Japanese pet magazine <u>Midori</u> <u>Shobo</u> *listing the winners (oranda calico class) of a goldfish competition.*

ounces of Epsom salts and one ounce of sodium bicarbonate as well. A temperature of 75°F. is best. The eggs hatch in one or two days. The shrimp can be fed on brewer's yeast.

I find brine shrimp to be one of the best foods, carrying no diseases and stimulating the activity of the fish.

Tubifex

This thin long red worm is found in swamp-like areas. As a food for growing fry, nothing can compare with it. The major objection is that they are sometimes said to carry disease. They can be purchased in aquarium shops and should be kept in shallow water under a dripping faucet for at least 12 hours before feeding. Since their culture at home is difficult I do not recommend it.

Microworms

These tiny worms, white to beige in color, can also be purchased at your pet shop with instructions on how to culture them with oatmeal and a few other ingredients. When fry have reached the two-week stage this serves as an excellent food. A word of caution: if the culture turns sour, throw it out; don't re-use the worms.

Drosophila

The fruitfly is now taking its place among the popular goldfish foods. It is small (about one-fourth inch) and easy to cultivate. Of the many varieties only the wingless (vestigial) is of practical use. Your culture must be kept closed to prevent any wild flies from entering.

A simple culture can be made by boiling water, adding it to agar agar, and then adding some mashed banana. It is put in a jar and allowed to jell. Then a few fruitflies are added. Within two weeks you will have fruitflies to feed to your fish. Several jars should be started so that a new supply is constantly available.

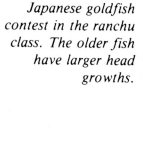

Winners of a Japanese goldfish contest in the ranchu class. The older fish have larger head growths.

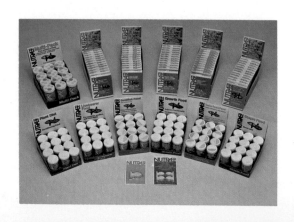

Prepared fish foods come in many different forms—flakes, pellets, granules, freeze-dried cubes, etc.

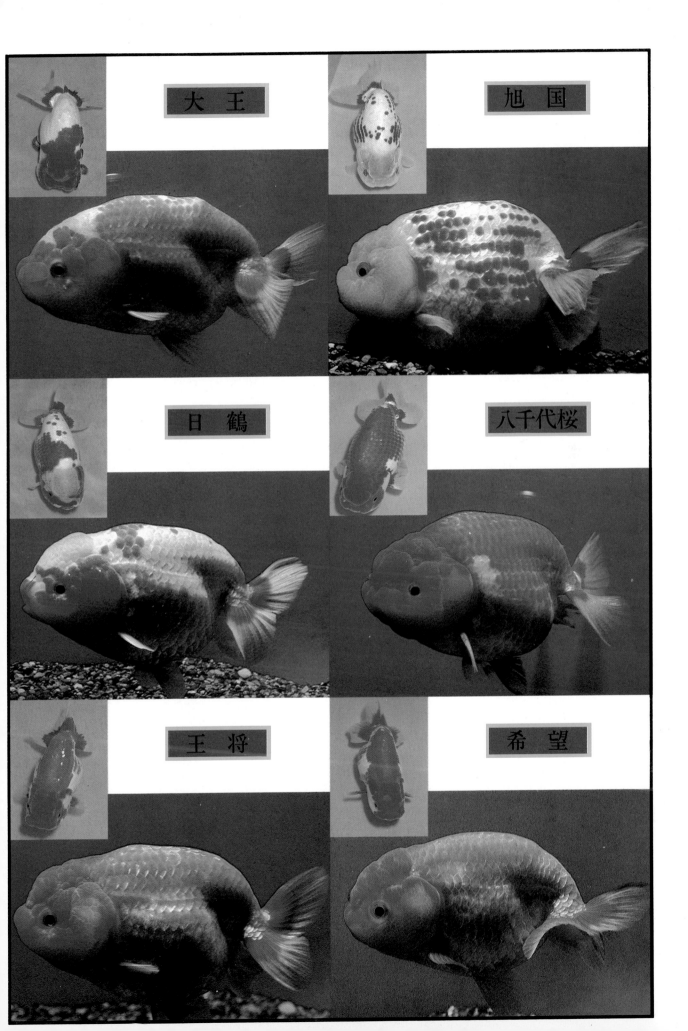

大　王

旭　国

日　鶴

八千代桜

王　将

希　望

Goldfish Foes

Many health problems derive from crowding, overfeeding, and fouling by waste materials. When any disease is identified it is as important to get rid of the source as it is to treat the fish. Disinfect the tank if more than one fish develops trouble.

On the following pages, I have charted common ailments and some ways to treat them. There are other methods but those given are the ones that I know work. Potassium permanganate and metallic copper are effective medications but they must be used with extreme caution. They can kill the fish they are supposed to cure. In most cases I do not recommend them to the novice. He is better off if he uses the reliable remedies purchasable at aquarium supply stores.

It is usually safe to assume that a diseased fish was weak before it was attacked. Most foes are airborne and will not attack a fish until its resistance is down. If you keep your tank clean, your fish healthy, and you isolate newcomers and perform periodic checks, you will rarely meet any of these problems. An ounce of prevention is always worth a pound of cure.

Wounds should be swabbed with 5% methylene blue every 12 hours for two days; this will keep fungus from taking hold.

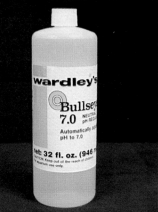

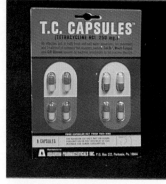

1. Chlorine remover. 2. pH stabilizer. 3. remedy for "ich." 4. aquarium antibiotics in capsule form.

FISH FOES

Name	Symptoms	Treatment
Gill Fluke (Dactylogyrus)	Gills swell up, with a pus-like substance exuded around the area. (Prevalent among fry.) Fish gasp for air.	Fish are placed in a 2-quart-container; 10 drops of formaldehyde are added to the water; then 10 more drops are added every minute for the next 10 minutes. If fish shows any discomfort remove it. Repeat daily for the next 3 days.

For fry, add 6 tblsp. of rock salt per quart of water. Dip fry in this for 30 seconds; then place them in a disinfected tank. Repeat in one hour for a final treatment. |
| Skin Fluke (Gyrodactylus) | Fish looks as if it has a fluffy coat on. It scratches continually and shows movements of irritation. | As above. |

DISEASES OF GOLDFISH

Fungused eggs.

Dropsy

Body fungus.

COLOR ABNORMALITIES

amelanotic

Tail-rot.

lutino

albino

A blind goldfish.

55

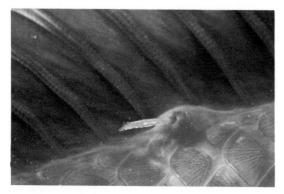

Anchor worm.

Dropsy.

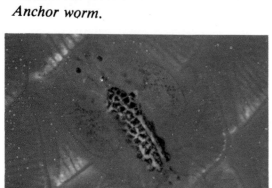

Fish louse.

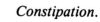

China disease.

Fish louse.

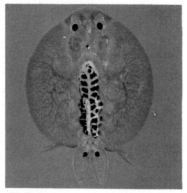

Fish louse.

Name	Symptoms	Treatment
Constipation or Indigestion	Fish is inactive; its abdomen bulges.	One tblsp. of Epsom salt in 5 gallons of water. Let fish fast for 4 days, then feed only live or frozen foods for one week.
Fish Lice (Argulus)	Violent rubbing to rid itself of parasite. A light green area about ⅛ inch in size will be noticed.	15-minute bath in a light pink solution of potassium permanganate. Remove parasite by placing a match on it or drip paraffin on it. Paint region with 5% methylene blue solution. Repeat paint job in 12 and 24 hours.
Anchor Worm (Lernaea)	Violent rubbing; scabs form; a white worm protrudes.	As above. Make sure you pick the worm out by its base, checking to see if you have the anchor. Disinfect your tank.
Dropsy	Bloated body; scales stand on end.	No known cure. Try a warm salt water bath for a day. If no response, destroy specimen.
Ich (Ichthyophthirius)	Fine pepper-like spots extending over body and fins.	5 drops of 5% methylene blue per gallon. Keep fish in it for one week. 4 drops of 2% Mercurochrome used instead of 5 drops of methylene blue.
Fin Rot or Tail Rot	Bad shredding of tips of fins, gradually moving inward. Shredding starts at edge and works in.	5-minute dip in a solution of 8 crystals of potassium permanganate to 3 quarts of water. Cut off ragged portion of fin with razor blade; paint stub with 5% methylene blue.
Fin Congestion	Blood vessels in fins become red and swollen. Later fins begin to split.	1 tblsp. rock salt in 1 gallon of water; fast fish in this for 4 days.
Fungus (Saprolegnia)	Fluffy white patches over body and fins.	1 tsp. salt in 3 quarts of water; keep fish in this one week, changing solution daily. One drop per gallon of 5% methylene blue – keeps fungus off eggs. Malachite green solution sold in stores.
China Disease	Varying from fraying or split fins which start near the base and work out to fin edge; sometimes blackening of fins and ventral region.	No known cure. Destroy fish and disinfect tank. Highly contagious.
Swim Bladder Problems	Fish, especially fancy ones, turn upside down with belly up.	If a female, it could be spawn binding. Rid her of eggs by pressing lightly on abdomen, working fingers toward anus. If not this, try a mild salt bath (1 tsp. per gallon). Many times this rights itself.

Beyond all else in keeping goldfish healthy, the aquarium should have daily cleaning if possible; if not, at least every other day. Decaying matter, an overabundance of algae, or just poor maintenance can lower the resistance of your fish until they are easy victims for their foes. A well-rounded diet of live food, frozen food, pastes, and dried preparations will do much to produce fine healthy fish, brighten their colors, and enhance their beauty. Every other month one tablespoon of aquarium salt for each ten gallons of water should be added to the tank to stimulate the fish and lessen the chances of infection. Extensive water changes and constant dipping of the hands into the tank should both be avoided.

An oranda with a narial bouquet.

A red head or red cap goldfish. This is one of the early specimens in the development of this beautiful variety.

A wakin goldfish, above. A calico, lower left; a shubunkin, lower right.

The fish shown on this page are the newest variety of goldfish, developed in Japan in 1980. The variety is called either "edojikin" or "kujaku," which means peacock.

Genetics

If you decide to breed goldfish, you must know something about that branch of biology known as genetics which deals with heredity and variation. During the last 40 years Professor Chen of China, Dr. Matsui of Japan, and Dr. Affleck of Great Britain have done much to clarify the confusing mass of facts concerning the heredity of goldfish.

Even before genetics became the vogue, Dr. Matsui set up a breeding schedule to stagger the imagination. Through thousands of spawnings he established a goldfish evolution flow which has stood the test of time.

Upon examining Matsui's work, you will notice two differently indicated lines. The solid lines represent direct mutations from the previous form. As an example: the first double-tailed mutation occurred in the common fish and, being selected for this, produced a strain known to the Japanese as the wakin, a long-bodied fish with a short double caudal fin. The dotted lines represent crosses where one type has been mated with another type. An example of this is the calico ryukin, which is said to be the product of a ryukin crossed with a sanshoku-demekin (calico telescope). The ranchu prototype had no hood, but the general body shape and finnage of the three that followed it looked basically like the osaka ranchu variety present today. The nankin has a fuller body and the downward-type tail.

A very beautiful and rare variety is the Chinese fish named after the city in which it originated, Nanking. The Japanese also name their fish after the city of origin; for example, "Edojikin" is a fish from Edo. (Edo is the old name for Tokyo).

When breeding goldfish, there are several things that will happen regularly, and for these we have a genetic explanation. Tail form tends to breed fairly true, and for that reason any fish that does not have a completely split caudal should not be bred. If a parent lacks an anal, this will probably show up in the next generation. A few broad generalizations can be made as to those traits inheritable most of the time. In goldfish there is a constant tendency toward reversion. A fancy goldfish can produce all culls if bred improperly or if it is just not a good breeder. The single caudal, dorsal fin, and elongated bodies will usually be dominant over any change from the normal common goldfish.

This leads us to the terms *dominant* and *recessive*. These genetic terms are used with goldfish but with some reserve. Because so many things can happen it is best to say that the *majority* will occur according to genetic theory. As an example:

On April 8 a female (♀) Calico Comet with black eyes and nacreous body was crossed with a male (♂) orange lionhead which belonged to the metallic scale group. If we take RR to mean metallic, Rr for nacreous, and rr to represent matt, we can illustrate it so:

♀ Rr × ♂ RR P₁ (meaning parent generation)

This cross should produce 50% metallics and 50% nacreous because if blocked out it reads as:

	R	R ♂
R	RR	RR
♀ r	Rr	Rr

In actuality, 35 metallic Comets were produced with 35 nacreous Comets with black eyes, 10 nacreous Comets with one black and one metallic eye, and 3 nacreous Comets with metallic eyes. The ratio of 35 : 48 is not bad and illustrates this point. It should be noted that *all* the fish exhibit a Comet body and finnage (singletail), have a dorsal fin, and have developed no hood after eight months of observation.

With something like telescope eyes, the normal eye is dominant, and a cross between a telescoped fish and a normal fish will usually produce normal-eyed fish which when bred in turn will prove that they were only apparently normal-eyed. This can be explained by considering two generations.

The word *homozygous* describes the type that has both factors the same, while *heterozygous* denotes the type which has one factor of the recessive and one factor of the dominant. If *EE* is used as the homozygous dominant trait of eyes, then *ee* represents the homozygous recessive trait of globe (telescope) eyes. As stated before, the heterozygote *Ee* has the dominant normal eye factor and therefore appears like a normal eye. Using the steps we set up before, our chart is as follows:

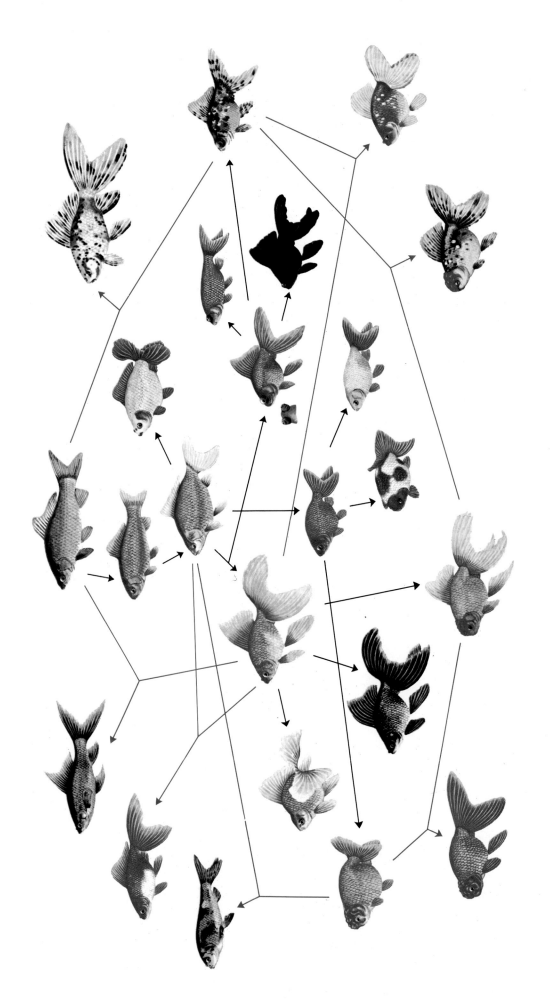

Dr. Yoshiichi Matsui's genetics chart, showing how the different varieties of Japanese goldfish developed. The red lines indicate crossings; the black lines indicate direct mutations.

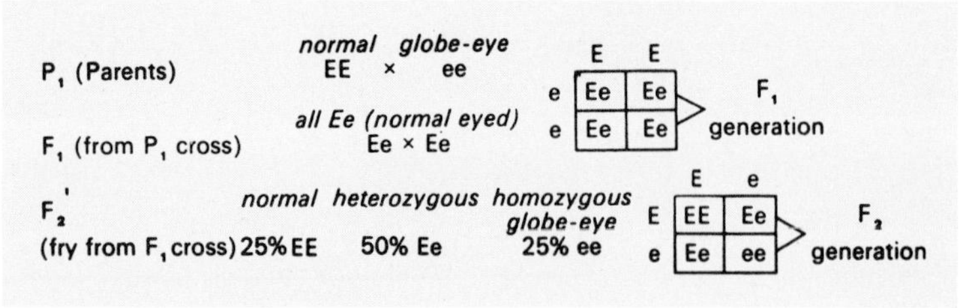
P$_1$ (Parents)
normal globe-eye
EE × ee
E E
e Ee Ee
e Ee Ee
F$_1$ generation
F$_1$ (from P$_1$ cross)
all Ee (normal eyed)
Ee × Ee
F$_2$
(fry from F$_1$ cross) 25% EE
normal heterozygous homozygous globe-eye
50% Ee
25% ee
E e
E EE Ee
e Ee ee
F$_2$ generation

On the facing page: A spawning orgy of goldfish.

Proper know-how in selecting the right breeders takes time and experience. Follow a set of standards in choosing the ones which best approach the ideal, and you stand a good chance of getting some better fish which, when bred, will produce offspring that may be even better. The coloration and body shape cycle in goldfish is about five years. Therefore it will take at least six generations (six years) before you know if you are on the right track. This is one reason why it is better to work with only one variety, trying different crosses.

Genetics is a highly complicated affair and certainly not one which can be gone into very thoroughly in a book this size. For further information or answers to specific questions our suggestion is that you consult the more detailed treatises on goldfish breeding which your dealer can recommend.

Very beautiful calico orandas.

ランチュウの産卵状況

Breeding and Raising

For each pair of fish being bred, you will need at least four tanks of 20-gallon capacity and one tank of at least 30-gallons. Thoroughly disinfect all of these tanks with a strong potassium permanganate solution or an ammonia solution if the ammonia does not contain detergent. When this has been done, place the 30-gallon in a spot where the first morning rays of the sun will strike it. Fill it up, add two tablespoons of salt, and let it stand. This will be your isolation and spawning tank.

Next prepare the four 20-gallon tanks, placing them in indirect light. Fill them about three-quarters full. I have found that covers over the tanks minimize the dust that accumulates on the bottom. This is vital for the fry because if too much accumulates the alevins can suffocate when they rest below. Heaters are necessary if you want to control the hatching time.

The next step is to select the pair which you desire to breed. Keep in mind the standards you have set, and under most circumstances do not choose any with poorly divided caudals or missing anals. Goldfish mature at one year but are in their prime about their third year. Some breeders prefer a two-year-old female with a three-year-old male; others say size should be considered; still another group recommends trios. I have tried all three methods and have come to the conclusion that there is little difference.

A male that is ready to spawn usually has tubercles or pearl organs, hard epidermal (skin) growths about pin-head in size. The tubercles usually appear on the operculum and first ray of the pectoral fin, but many times they can be found on other fins. It is possible that some males will not develop them, and under unusual circumstances some females have been known to sprout them. In nacreous and matt fish the testis, a long white organ, can be observed in the male fish just above the coiled intestines, which are brown. Some breeders say that during the breeding season (spring and summer) the male's body is elongated and narrows near the tail. If you turn the fish over you may notice that the anal region in a male is elongated and very distinct.

The female fills out during the breeding season, making shape the primary method of sexing her. In matt and nacreous goldfish, the granular yellow ovaries loaded with eggs can easily be observed. The female's body becomes rounded and, especially in long-bodied varieties, lopsidedness will be spotted. The anal region is ovoid and not very distinct. Once you are pretty sure she is a female with roe feel her belly and check if it is soft and firm. A firm feeling tells you that she is almost ready to spawn.

Newly laid goldfish eggs are sticky and adhere to the leaves of fine-leaved plants.

Once the pair has been chosen, give them a dip in light pink solution of potassium permanganate for three hours. Maintain them in your 30-gallon for five days but keep them separated with a divider. Repeat this treatment five days later; in the meantime disinfect the 30-gallon and refill it with water from one of the 20-gallons. Refill this 20-gallon tank so it is ready for use later. Continue to keep the two fish separated in a dimly lit area. Feed them plenty of live food and vegetable matter but do *not* feed them powdered or flaked foods. Temperature should vary from 70°F. during the day to 50°F. at night. After one week of this conditioning, take out the divider and add the spawning grass. An excellent spawning media is a nylon spawning mop; it should be rinsed and sterilized before being placed in the tank.

You will notice a few false starts, but after a day or two the spawning chase will begin in earnest. After driving the female for two or three hours, the male begins bumping her abdomen. If she is ready, eggs will spurt out and adhere to the first thing they touch. They are usually released in batches, the first batch being the best. The buck (male) fertilizes the eggs immediately by spraying milt over them. Good-sized females will lay from 500-1000 eggs a spawn.

Remove the eggs immediately and rinse them in a bucket of aged water of the *same* temperature. (Important: goldfish spawn as the water warms in the morning sun, so be standing by when the first morning rays of sunlight strike the tank.) After a quick rinse place the eggs in the 20-gallon tanks, distributing them so that there are about 15 eggs per gallon of water.

At this point raise the temperature in the holding tanks to about 70°F. The fish will hatch in three or four days. By the end of the first day you will notice some eggs are clear tan to yellow while others are white. Those which are almost clear are fertile; the others are infertile and will probably be attacked by fungus. The white eggs should be removed without delay. Some breeders have luck with a few drops of methylene blue in these tanks to cut down the occurrence of fungus.

The alevin hatches out along the region of his back, pulling his tail out first, then moving it quickly to release his head. A birth he is about a sixteenth to an eighth inch long and has two large black eyes, a long notochord, and a full yolk sac. These translucent fry should not be disturbed. Don't be alarmed if they fall to the bottom. Within 48 hours after hatching they will have absorbed their yolk sacs and an air bladder and rudimentary pectoral fin will become noticeable.

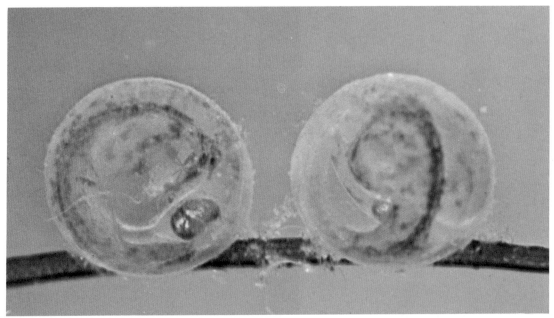

1

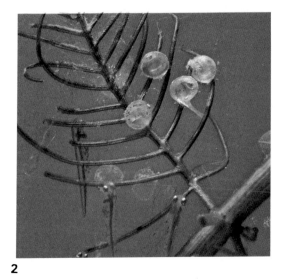

2

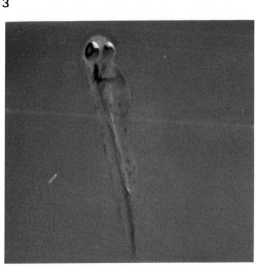

3

1. Eggs about 3 days old. The eggs will hatch within 24 hours. Eggs hatch at about 96 hours of age in water about 70°F. 2. Eggs as they hatch. Some fry pop out of the egg as sticky little fish while others just have their tails protruding through the egg case. 3. An egg at the instant of hatching 4. After a few days of being ''sticky'' the fry finally become free-swimming. At the free-swimming stage they will have absorbed their yolk sacs and will be searching for microscopic foods.

4

The feeding schedule should be as follows:

After 48 hours	Crushed yolk of hardboiled egg and oatmeal paste or, for the beginner, fry liquid as produced commercially.
After 2 weeks	Baby brine shrimp and infusoria.
After 3 weeks	Powdered foods can be added.
First 4 weeks	Feed 3 times daily.
Up to 4 months	Feed 2 times daily.
After 4 months	Once a day.

(Feedings should be as much as they can eat in 20 minutes.)

Always siphon off excess food, taking care not to draw up any fry. Once a month add a tablespoon of salt to the tank. Artificial aeration can be provided after one month. At one month cull down to 30 fry in each tank, discarding any fish which are misshapen in body or finnage. This culling should be done with a spoon or cup, *never* with a net. When the fish have reached half-inch, they should be separated into two sizes. The faster growers will starve the others if they are not taken away. When the fish reach one inch they should be culled for body shape and split finnage. This time the thinning should leave six to eight fish in each tank. Cull at the end of four months, leaving only three fish in each tank. At the age of one year, the final cull takes place, picking the four best who will become your breeders for the following year.

It has been said that alga-filled water and feeding starches to fry which develop hoods later on retard or even suppress the growth of the hood. Live foods are to be preferred, along with clear water.

Mr. F. L. Vanderplank of Great Britain recommends a color formula of: one crystal of manganese sulphate, one crystal of nickel sulphate, one crystal of potassium bichromate, and a tiny portion (half the size of a rice grain) of copper sulphate, all dissolved in a quart of water, mixing well. Two or three drops (no more) of this solution added per ten gallons of water every two weeks are supposed to bring out the color of the fry. A slightly alkaline tank toughens the fry's skin, making it hardier.

Young fish which have not grown to at least two inches by October should be wintered indoors. Some breeders take in their best specimens and first year fish so that they can be carefully watched.

Experimentation is important at all times because different parts of the world present varying conditions and climates. It will be necessary for you to learn by experience the breeding methods which are best for you.

Artificial spawning is not for the novice. It has both advantages and disadvantages. Professional breeders disagree on its use. Until you have mastered the techniques of natural spawning, don't even attempt any artificial method.

Pearl-scaled goldfish are one of the more beautiful varieties of goldfish. The old fish above and the younger fish shown to the left are one of Nature's few scale variations in fishes. As far as is known, only carp and goldfish have scale deformities which have been inbred. None of the usual aquarium fishes are known to have anything like "pearl" scales except the goldfish.

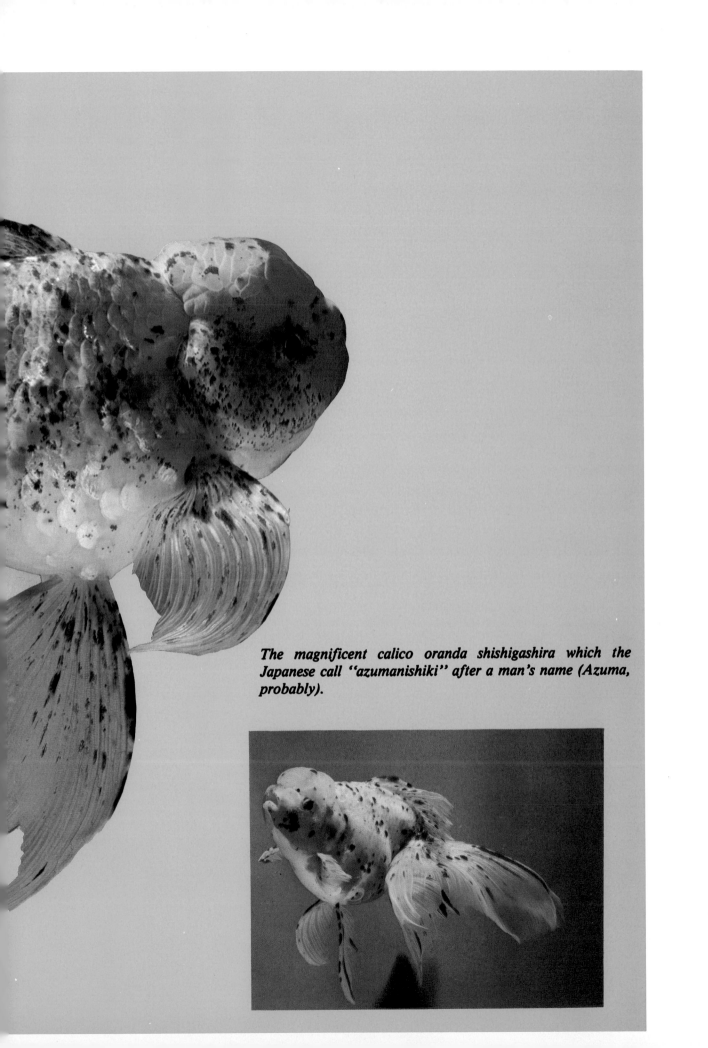

The magnificent calico oranda shishigashira which the Japanese call "azumanishiki" after a man's name (Azuma, probably).

Standards and Shows

The novice goldfish keeper who is just starting out in all probability will not be interested in showing fish. He should, however, be aware of the standards when purchasing his fish, not only to obtain the best possible specimens but also should he some day decide to breed them.

As stated earlier, standards are only guides, and not everyone agrees with them. The Japanese do not go by Chinese standards, nor do the Americans follow the British system. National pride as well as varying tastes make each breeder his own judge. Basic to any standard is the setting of a goal one step beyond the possible perfect in each fish. The joy in breeding is to try to come as close to perfection as possible.

In 1963, the Goldfish Society of Great Britain set up a new set of standards with the idea of maintaining types originally produced and not hybrids of others. Their set makes a good starting point.

In single-tailed fish the body should be long and thin. The double-tailed types with a dorsal have very shortened bodies which add to their gracefulness. Double-tailed variations without a dorsal are a little longer and have short fins instead of large ones which would be detrimental to the fish's welfare. Incompletely split caudals, lack of anals, and disfiguration of fins are immediate forms of disqualifications.

On the facing page is the typical report on a Japanese goldfish show. It has three champions and three second prize winners in each of the following categories: One Year Olds; Two Year Olds; Adults (any age). The comments about each fish are poetic. The second prize winner in the Two Year Old Section reads as follows: Kikuhomare. There is no need to explain the beauty of this fish since the picture speaks for itself. This fish swims like a young shark. It has color, beauty and demeanor which is appreciated most by the most serious of goldfish fanciers. The fish has strength (merit) because of its contrasting brilliant redness. The red eye and the red spot on the snout remind one of the former champion Nonukichi Sotoyama. The excellent characteristics of the former champion must have been passed on to this fish from the champion's daughter. *Because of its relatively small body, the fish only won a second prize.*

A 1978 variety known as the "feather dress."

御殿桜
■親魚の部／1席
岡崎・深津隆一氏持魚

　審査会の当日、会員及び観覧者の待ちわびる中へ1席の魚がはこびこまれた。たくましさと美しさを兼ねそなえていて、尚且つ泳ぎもいい。赤紅色の色彩もまたあざやかである。腰が太いので尾を上手にこなして泳ぐ。頭から口に下る線の伸びやかさや、また肩から背ビレに至るみごとな線。これだけ雄大さと力感と味わいをそれぞれにみせながらも、各ヒレの洗いが少ない事は素質もあろうし、飼育者の日頃の丹精は言葉につくしきれないものがある。越冬後の稚魚の作出に全力を尽されたいと願うものである。魚名の如く、御殿桜として衆人にあがめられる名魚である。

花吹雪
■親魚の部／2席
岡崎・深津隆一氏持魚

　1席、2席は兄弟魚であろう。魚味が実によく似たところを持っている。これも立派な魚であった。太さから来るものだけ言うならば、桜吹雪の方に力はあるが、全般の総合力に於て御殿桜を優位に見るべきであろう。この魚の方が背ビレと尾ビレの洗いが1席の魚よりもやや多い感じもあり、少差で2席となったが、1、2席を共にもつ所有者は、よろこびにたえない事と想像する。

王　冠
■2才魚の部／1席
岡崎・下川廣治氏持魚

　一番晴姿をみせる2才魚である。写真をみての通り、誠に精悍さを身につけて泳ぐ魚である。尾は裏皿が大きくえぐれた尾形にふさわしい力のいい形状である。頭部は小さいが目先は長く品位にあふれ、鱗がこまかく非常によいものをみせている。赤紅の色彩も十分でありながら、全くと言ってよい程各ヒレの洗いをみせない。魚は太いがゆるみがなく、しまった太さである。飼育者はこの魚が雄魚である事を承知していて、特に心して飼っているので、その立派さは一段である。

貴久誉
■2才魚の部／2席
西尾・外山すみゑ氏持魚

　この写真をみれば下手な説明は必要ないかも知れない。水中の遊泳は実に若い鯱を思わせる。味、味、味、である。玄人に尊ばれるよさをみせる。力感は申すまでもない。色彩も濃く又ヒレの洗いもない。赤い眼と鼻に紅を残してあるのも、先代外山信吉をしのぶ。この魚1尾をみても先代が嫁に伝えた汗と血のにおいが筆者の心をゆすぶってならない。やや体が小さいために2席となってしまった。

藤　娘
■当才魚の部／1席
岡崎・犬塚　清氏持魚

　当才にしてこのような魚が出来るようになった事は、保存会として嬉しいことである。当才ながらいかにも充実した姿をみせている。腹の切れ上りから腰の太さ、短さ、尾のエグレ、裏皿の大きさ、左右均等等の力のある尾形、頭部も胴部もまた立派なものである。保存会を設立するとき、設立委員達が考えたすえ書いた栞の画の体形に非常によくにている。尾形はその画に比べれば当才だからやや違っているが、何としても高度の価値ある魚である。

房　錦
■当才魚の部／2席
名古屋・小島房和氏持魚

　1席の魚と兄弟である。非常によく似ている。この2尾は三河地方の各会で共によく出品され、必ずというほど1、2席とならんだ魚で、その席は「兄たりがたく、弟たりがたし」で、互に1席をとりあった魚である。然し、総決算ともいうべき特別優秀魚指定審査会にて、遂に雌雄を決してしまった。審査会の当日の判断は審査員の判断通りである。前者に比してやや魚が硬さがなかった点に1席に立てなかった。この2尾のみでなく、数多くの立派な当才魚を育てた犬塚氏に讃辞をおくりたい。

Outdoor Ponds

The topic of outdoor ponds for goldfish is big enough to require a full-sized book. We mention them at all only because goldfish are the usual denizens of these pools. Almost all the varieties can be kept outside during the breeding season. A breeding-size goldfish should be outside for at least two months a year. This gives them the needed vigor they can acquire in no other way. In fact, if you do not want to spawn your goldfish in tanks, just leave them in an outdoor pond and nature will take its course.

Aquatic plants, water lilies, and bog plants all add to the glamor of a well-stocked and planned garden pool. Night varieties of water lilies and tall lotus plants give goldfish an environment well suited for their health.

Fish should not be wintered in any pond less than three feet deep; it should never be so shallow that the water can freeze solidly at the bottom.

Besides goldfish, the golden orfe and Crucian carp provide interesting additions to an outside pond. The Japanese koi or higoi is another type of fish with interesting colors. Although body-shape mutations of the koi have not yet occurred, their coloring far surpasses that of goldfish. People with outdoor ponds should seriously consider adding this attractive variety to their pools.

Blue goldfish.

A Last Few Words

In closing, let me re-emphasize three things. Experimentation—and that means trial and error—is the only way to good fishkeeping. Caution and precaution are the greatest assets. A reliable pet shop dealer can be your best friend.

There are many regional groups which welcome novices interested in raising and breeding goldfish. Check with your local pet shop dealer for the address of one in your area. Meeting other hobbyists can do much to broaden your knowledge and increase your interest.

Brown goldfish.

Red cap or red head.

A beautiful outdoor goldfish pond. Photo courtesy of Van Ness.